How to Profit with TikTok

by

ken Douglas

Table of Contents

What is TikTok and Who is Using It for Business?

TikTok is a video sharing social networking service that has been available in the United States since 2016. It uses short-form videos anywhere from fifteen seconds to one minute long in a wide variety of categories including, but not limited to, dance, comedy, and education. The videos tend to be a hybrid between entertainment and *info*tainment depending on what you're looking for.

TikTok is available world-wide and currently there are 40 languages you can tap into for the service. While TikTok is not the only platform designed to share short videos, there is something about the app that is setting itself apart from others. Here are some fun facts about TikTok and the people who use it-

Fun Facts About TikTok

- **Fun Fact:** 50% of users are under the age of 34
- **Fun Fact:** Content ranges on the scale from raw, real, funny, to shocking
- **Fun Fact:** The average TikTok user is on 52 minutes per day
- **Fun Fact:** 60% of users are female
- **Fun Fact:** 26% of users are 18-24
- **Fun Fact:** Millennials and Boomers are adding the TikTok app at an alarming rate

TikTok is More Than Dancing and Comedy Bits

Tiktok is much more than fifteen seconds of dance moves. In many ways, TikTok is taking the lead in producing influencers. TikTok "influencers" seem to go viral with alarming speed and often times see a surge in their followers over night from a single video.

The app is ever evolving, and new categories are beginning and growing all the time including alternative lifestyle categories, DIY and upcycling, business, and behind-the-scenes looks at industries typically off-limits to insider information.

Who is Using TikTok?

The stats suggest most of the users are between 18-35 but those numbers are changing every day as every age group enjoys the benefits of TikTok. Though it is certainly entertaining, it is also a smart business tool. In the past year TikTok has generated millions of dollars in revenue for its users in a wide variety of ways. From being an influencer to linking to goods and services, the potential to earn via TikTok is pretty amazing since there is not cost associated with the platform.

In the end, there's no drawback to TikTok. The learning curve for making videos is fairly easy and the potential to generate revenue is easier and cheaper than other platforms that use ads like Facebook or Instagram. Having an account is as easy as downloading the app and since it's been around a while, there are plenty of tutorials on how to maximize your account.

TikTok is a relatively new social networking platform that may be a smart business move to get noticed and make money.

Not all Profit is $- Hidden Resources on the TikTok App

When it comes to business, the bottom line tends to be profit. Why else would you be in business if it isn't to make money? Well, not all profit is money. Sometimes there are hidden resources that are as good as...*or better,* than money.

TikTok has the potential to create a buzz about you and your goods and services. These can lead to resources that you may not have imagined. Some TikTok influencers have seen rampant and unexpected benefits that have incredible value. Take a look-

Mikayla Nogueira- Makeup artist influencer: Mikayla started out on TikTok simply as someone who loves makeup. She began an Instagram account sharing tutorials in 2013 and only gained 43k followers. On TikTok she has amassed over 3.7 Million followers. Since coming to TikTok, she has earned over a million in income, products and other goods and services.

Mikayla has not only monetized her TikTok account she has benefitted from hidden resources like free products, collaborations, and exposure to people in her industry she would not otherwise been able to access. She is now beginning to branch out into other areas of interest to her followers including mental health issues she manages.

DogFace- One TikTok account took the world by storm with a simple video showcasing Nathan Apodaca drinking Ocean Spray cranberry juice cocktail while riding a skateboard with Fleetwood Mac's Dreams playing in the background. The back story was his car broke down on the way to work and he simply wasn't going to let his situation get the best of him. Well, his zen-like attitude catapulted him to TikTok fame triggering a series of copy-cat videos with some pretty famous people. Ultimately, he was given a new truck from Ocean Spray after his video caused a spike in consumption of their product.

While the majority of videos do not go viral, many do. It isn't unusual to get thousands of views on videos and the ratio of influencers on TikTok tends to be higher than other platforms as in Mikayla's case where she had infinitely more traction on TikTok than Instagram.

While it is possible to earn income from TikTok, some people link their Venmo and other cash app accounts, there are also other benefits that may not translate to dollars in your bank account but can be equally lucrative. Here are some benefits you may not want to pass up-

- **Merchandise from companies you endorse**
- **Collaborations with other influencers**
- **Donations**
- **Growing accounts and selling them**

There are a lot of possibilities to generate income and other resources from TikTok.

Developing your account could lead to a profitable experience.

Make Friends and Collab- The Power of Partnerships

TikTok is a social networking platform. That means it relies on engagement for its success. Having a successful account is great, but one of the cool elements of TikTok is the ability to collaborate with other creators on their TikTok accounts.

"Stitch" Your Way to Powerful Partnerships

Stitching is a TikTok term that describes stitching together two TikToks. Generally, this is a way to highlight another account and add to or provide commentary. This can be especially beneficial if done in a strategic way. TikTok users often use stitching as a way to gain access to people they may not otherwise have under ordinary circumstances. It is considered flattering to stitch someone's content and rude not to respond.

One account, @angryreactions, became wildly successful achieving 4 million followers in record-breaking time. His seemingly angry reactions to benign things are, in fact, heartfelt supportive reactions that surprise the viewer. His account has been stitched by a wide range of artists and other creators who have made things in his likeness. Stitching their accounts to his gives them potential exposure to his 4 million followers for themselves. This can enhance their opportunities for their work to be seen simply by giving his account attention and stitching to his.

The Power of Comments Enhances the Fun

TikTok is unique in that many users highlight comments made on their videos and use them in creative ways. One trend that is popular is calling out negative people and putting them on blast. This turns the tables on trolls or bullies and calls them out publicly for their negativity. Commentary in the comments section of a video can, in and of itself, become content. This can lead to some fun collaborations and build powerful partnerships that may be leveraged down the line. Leaving a witty and/or powerful comment on a popular account may have direct benefits to yours.

Collaborating is a Two-Way Street

Getting in on the fun and making friends is a two-way street. If you are starting out, you may not know too many people nor have the clout that some accounts have. The great thing about TikTok is things can happen quickly. If you create great content, stitch wisely, and engage with other accounts, the likelihood you'll get noticed increases. Networking on TikTok is a lot like networking at a business convention or meetup. The more active you are, the more impressive and interesting you'll be to others.

Building your presence on TikTok can help you find more followers and increase your chances of making friends and collaborating. Collaborations can help build your exposure and platform rapidly. This can lead to more people linking to your website or other resources. In the end, it's simply good practice to be an active part of the community as you use it for your business.

Host TikTok Lives to Build Know, Like, and Trust

TikTok is a social networking platform where content producers can share anything they want. It's quite remarkable how varied the content is which is delivered by an ever-changing algorithm that learns more and more about you and your interests during each session.

TikTok has two feeds that supply videos to your app. The *For You* feed are suggested accounts that you may have interest in based on your preferences or past viewing habits. Your *Following* feed is filled with accounts you are subscribed to that have released fresh content. You can toggle back and forth between the two with ease.

Focus on High-Quality, Consistent Content to Build Your Platform

When creating an account, the focus should be on high-quality content that is consistent with your brand and delivered on a routine basis. The two can lead to a large and engaging following. When it comes to using TikTk for business and generating income, the focus should be on content that is logical to your followers. Since they may find your account from their *For You* feed, they may make the decision to follow you, *or not,* based on one encounter. That means if your account is geared towards education about a topic or teaching a technique and you release a random video about tuna fish, you may lose a potential ideal follower for your account.

For best results, your account should host videos that are consistent with your message. If you are teaching about a subject, stick with it and don't get off subject or you may confuse or lose followers.

Use TikTok Live to Build the Know, Like, and Trust Factor

Once you've established yourself as an expert or entertainer, you can boost your credibility and the fanfare of your account by hosting TikTok lives. These are live feeds where your followers can engage with you in real time and ask questions or see a side of you they may not see in the video content.

TikTok lives are a great way to show your personality outside of your business persona or to build relationships with the people who are following you. Giving them shout outs, undivided attention, or otherwise engaging with them can make you more appealing and set you apart. This can help you reach many people at one time and increase their impression of you and their willingness to work with you, buy your products or merchandise.

The TikTok live feature is a wonderful way to engage with your followers and increase how much they know about you, like, you and trust what you have to say. It's an excellent investment in shifting followers from watchers to customers.

Link to your Etsy Shop, Website, and Other Links that Make you Money

There are a lot of ways to profit from a solid TikTok account. Some content creators aren't technically in it for business, but they have such loyal and rabid fans that they often receive "happy mail" or donations to encourage them to keep creating. Ultimately, some of the most popular content creators end up creating "merch" or *branded products* to offer their followers. Whether you use TikTok for personal or business use, there are a lot of ways to use your profile for profits.

Your Bio Is Important Real Estate

Your bio is an important part of your TikTok account. You can list a brief description of your qualifications, intent for your account or anything that helps a follower identify you and what you do. You can also link to your Instagram account or a website. Choose your links carefully to make sure they lead to the most profitable ways to connect.

Share Links to your Money-Making Sources

Etsy- If you are a creator, Etsy is a great way to drive followers to your goods. You can easily create TikToks of yourself creating something and encourage followers to head to your Etsy account to place an order.

Website- If you have multiple resources, link to your website and create a landing page with other links to your business assets. From one link your followers can access a variety of links or a landing page with one call to action.

Linktree or LIKEtoKNOW.it- These platforms offer you a way to direct followers to content you have affiliate links for. These are great for apps like TikTok and Instagram that only allow one link in the bio. You can use your social networking platform to generate a buzz or excitement about products you use and give followers a way to buy them, earning you a commission and passive income.

Important note: Not all links will be available to every account. Some links require a minimum of 1000 followers or more before you can use some commission-based links. The good news is, TikTok has lower follower minimums than other platforms like Instagram. Use your account in the meantime to build your followers and share valuable content so you reach the minimum number of subscribers fast.

You can utilize the bio section of your TikTok account to create access to more information about you and your business and offer opportunities to profit. Be strategic with your bio. Make sure it's catchy, informative, and shares the information that gives you credibility and sets you apart from other creators.

Tips to Set Up Your TikTok for Financial Success

If you're a newbie to TikTok, that could be a very good thing. If you haven't set up your account, you are in a perfect position to get proper information that sets your account up for financial success.

Starting from scratch can be advantageous so you can set about building your TikTok account from the ground up intentionally. Though the platform is educational, informational, and entertaining, it can also be a source of profit. Here's how to set your account up for financial success.

- **Determine your USP**
- **Create a content plan**
- **Use your bio to its fullest capacity**
- **Focus on delivering high-quality content**
- **Be consistent and creative**
- **Commit to the long game**

Determine your USP- Your *Unique Selling Proposition* or focus for your account is very important. Be sure that what you intend to create is something you can create content for over time. Narrow your niche so you are serving a specific targeted audience. One creator @suzieedge is a physician and historian who uses a mashup model of sharing education and infotainment to get people excited about medieval medical conditions.

Create a content plan- Having a strategic plan beats winging it. Making a content plan can help you build know, like, and trust, with your followers and give you a guide for how you want to build up your content over time that leads to followers taking actions towards a profitable level.

Use your bio to its full potential- The bio is a great way to link to your website, sales page, linktree, or LIKEtoKNOW.it. These can be important links for passive income and to help people connect with you outside of TikTok.

Focus on your content- Content should be meaningful and valuable. Think of it as a freemium. Share take-aways, tips, and tricks that are actionable so you build credibility and a relationship.

Be Consistent with your content- Be consistent with your content and resist going off into a new direction that might confuse your followers. If your account is about medieval medical conditions, don't throw in a random video about what you had for dinner. The most successful accounts are consistent with predictable but entertaining and informational content.

Commit to the long game- Building an account takes time. Be consistent and confident in your approach. If you happen to gain momentum quickly, that's awesome but for most people, slow and steady wins the race. If you get bored or quit too soon you may miss out on a lot of profits.

You can intentionally build your TikTok account to gain momentum and monetize if you are strategic and plan things out. Be intentional and consistent and you'll see amazing results that lead to amazing profits.

In the End, Be Sure to do THIS One Thing!

A TikTok account is a smart business tool and can create profitable connections, content, and collaborations. It's important to be business-minded when using any tool. Making important business decisions will ensure your time on TikTok is targeted to your ideal customer. Your efforts should be serious but, in the end, they should also be FUN!

If you spend much time on TikTok you'll definitely sense that the content creators who have fun tend to do the best. Creators who use humor, are pleasant, and genuinely enjoy the connection with their followers tend to have the highest numbers of followers and see more loyalty from their tribe. Creators who are negative, critical, or use humor in cringe-worthy ways may get a laugh or two, but followers don't tend to stick around for long.

You Can Have Fun Doing Anything

TikTok creators have proven that you can have a blast talking about anything. Some of the TikTokers in the medical field use humor to talk about troubling issues in positive ways. Other TikTokers use unique and entertaining ways to share information that are out-of-the-box which attracts more followers. TikTok is incredibly creative and proves you can find fun ways to talk about anything.

Find opportunities to share your information in fun and unique ways. Your followers will reward your efforts and it will make creating videos more fun for you as well. Even TikToks about proper grammar can have a fun, yet educational take on them.

Be Supportive to the Community

TikTok is a community. Have fun supporting other creators and engaging with them. Build relationships with TikTokers in your field and show your interest in their success. All ships rise in a high tide.

Be a fan too! Find TikTok accounts that you love for personal and business reasons. Comment, engage with them, and be part of what makes the TikTok community unlike any other social networking platform.

If you Don't Have Fun, you Won't Do It

In life, it's hard to do the things that aren't fun. If creating content isn't fun, you'll likely stop. Be sure to consider what's a good fit for your personality or your industry and promote your information in the best, *and most fun way,* possible.

If you're unsure how you can create fun and engaging content, spend time watching how-to videos or get some coaching or consulting. TikTok's been around long enough that there are creators out there who can teach you how to make content your tribe will love.

TikTok is one of many tools you can use to build a platform, support your other platforms, and engage a new audience. It's a simple and fun way to share content and help people find your resources. In the end, the most important thing is to have fun while serving your tribe.